Jack Russell
Terriers

ABDO
Publishing Company

A Buddy Book
by
Julie Murray

VISIT US AT
www.abdopub.com

Published by Buddy Books, an imprint of ABDO Publishing Company, 4940 Viking Drive, Suite 622, Edina, Minnesota 55435. Copyright © 2005 by Abdo Consulting Group, Inc. International copyrights reserved in all countries. No part of this book may be reproduced in any form without written permission from the publisher.

Printed in the United States.

Edited by: Christy DeVillier
Contributing Editors: Matt Ray, Michael P. Goecke
Graphic Design: Maria Hosley
Image Research: Deborah Coldiron
Photographs: American Kennel Club, Corbis, Getty Images, Photodisc, Photospin

Library of Congress Cataloging-in-Publication Data

Murray, Julie, 1969-
    Jack Russell terriers/Julie Murray.
        p. cm. — (Animal kingdom. Set II)
    Contents: The dog family — Jack Russell terriers — What they're like — Coat and color — Size — Care — Feeding — Things they need — Puppies.
    ISBN 1-59197-321-X
       1. Jack Russell terrier—Juvenile literature. [1. Jack Russell terrier. 2. Terriers. 3. Dogs.] I. Title.

SF429.J27M87 2003
636.755—dc21

                                        2002034549

Contents

Dogs

People have kept dogs for thousands of years. Millions of people have pet dogs today.

Many people enjoy keeping pet dogs.

The American Kennel Club has named about 150 dog **breeds**. Some breeds, such as German shepherds, are big dogs. Other breeds, such as toy poodles, are small dogs. Dogs from different breeds look different from each other. But all dogs belong to the Canidae family.

Jack Russell Terriers

Jack Russell terriers are also called Parson Russell terriers. They are named after Reverend John Russell. He lived in the 1800s. Reverend Russell trained his terriers to hunt foxes with him. Today, Jack Russell terriers are popular pets in the United States, Ireland, and England.

Jack Russell terriers are popular pets today.

What They Look Like

Jack Russell terriers are small dogs. They grow to become as tall as 15 inches (38 cm). Adults weigh between 13 and 17 pounds (6 and 8 kg).

Jack Russell terriers have strong bodies. They have long heads with almond-shaped eyes. A Jack Russell terrier's coat is mostly white. They have tan and black marks, too.

A Jack Russell terrier's coat is mostly white.

What They Are Like

Jack Russell terriers are smart, playful, and loving. They enjoy being near people.

Jack Russell terriers enjoy being with people.

Jack Russell terriers are active dogs. They are happy living in apartments or houses. But they need space to run and play. Jack Russells love to hunt, dig, and explore. They are good at jumping, too. Jack Russells can easily jump over a four-foot (one-m) fence.

Grooming And Care

Dogs need **grooming**. Brushing a dog's coat keeps it smooth and clean. Jack Russell terriers need to be brushed once a week.

Dogs need their nails clipped short. Cleaning a dog's teeth and ears is also important. Ask a **veterinarian** how to do this.

A **veterinarian** is a doctor for animals. Taking pets to a veterinarian helps them stay healthy. Dogs should visit a veterinarian about once a year.

13

Feeding And Exercise

All dogs need food and fresh water every day. Adult Jack Russell terriers should be fed once a day. Try not to change your dog's food too often. A changing **diet** can lead to health problems.

Dogs need food and water every day.

Jack Russell terriers enjoy playing with toys.

Dogs need exercise. Jack Russell terriers enjoy activity. They love running, swimming, and going on walks. Jack Russells enjoy games of chase and tug-of-war. Owners should play with their pets every day.

A Jack Russell terrier puppy

Puppies

Jack Russell terriers commonly have **litters** of four puppies. The puppies are born blind and deaf. They drink their mother's milk. Puppies will begin seeing and hearing at about two weeks old.

Puppies take naps between playtimes.

Puppies should stay with their mothers for eight weeks. Jack Russell terriers may live as long as 15 years.

Becoming the owner of a puppy is exciting. Caring for a puppy also means training it. Some people train their dogs with help from puppy schools. There, puppies learn to obey their owners. They learn commands like "sit" and "stay."

Dog Facts

❑ Dogs have been around for as long as 13,000 years.

❑ A dog's hearing is better than a person's hearing.

❑ Some dogs are trained to find fungi called truffles.

❑ Greyhounds can run as fast as 45 miles (72 km) per hour.

❑ The oldest dog on record lived to be 29 years old.

Important Words

breed a special group of dogs. Dogs of the same breed look alike.

diet the food that a dog (or a person) normally eats.

groom to clean and care for.

litter the group of puppies born at one time.

veterinarian a doctor for animals. A short name for veterinarian is "vet."

Web Sites

To learn more about Jack Russell terriers, visit ABDO Publishing Company on the World Wide Web. Web sites about Jack Russell terriers are featured on our Book Links page. These links are routinely monitored and updated to provide the most current information available.

www.abdopub.com

Index